My Little Blue House

A LIFE-AFTER-LOVE STORY

HEIDI DIXON

ILLUSTRATIONS
BY COLEEN BRADFIELD

ELECTRIC
MOON
PUBLISHING

Copyright 2023 by Heidi Dixon
Published through Electric Moon Publishing, LLC
©2023 My Little Blue House: A Life-After-Love Story / Heidi Dixon

Paperback ISBN: 978-1-7348037-7-8
E-book ISBN: 978-1-7348037-8-5

Electric Moon Publishing, LLC
P.O. Box 466
Stromsburg, NE 68666
info@emoonpublishing.com

SEL010000 SELF-HELP / Death, Grief, Bereavement
SEL021000 SELF-HELP / Motivational & Inspirational

Illustrations by Coleen Bradfield

Cover and Interior Design by Lyn Rayn / Electric Moon Publishing Creative Services

For questions contact mylittlebluehouse@outlook.com

Printed in the United States of America
ELECTRIC
MOON
PUBLISHING
www.emoonpublishing.com

AUTHOR'S NOTE

This story is about the intensely personal and universal experience of grief. It is based on the very real lived experiences of thirty-plus members of "Until We Meet Again," a weekly grief support group for anyone who has lived through the death of his or her spouse.

I started this group years ago. The hope, stories, and friendships have created a life of their own. Those who attend offer healing, perspective, and inspiration to one another and have done the same for me. I think they can do the same for you, which is why this book exists.

SPECIAL THANKS

A special thanks to my parents for the gift of life and for nourishing it in faith; my husband, Brett, who has insisted for years that I have a book in me; to my sister, Michelle, and friend Stacey, who have been champions for this project and in life; and to Deacon Dave, whose first question at every breakfast meeting has been "Have you found a publisher yet?"

DEDICATION

For my friends who meet every Monday at 11:00. You are my inspiration— teachers, heroes, editors, and marriage therapists. You have learned (and continue to learn) how to live without your spouses, all while not knowing how. What courage and love I see in you!

We are all made to be seen, heard, known, loved, and understood. This is for you, for all who know the little blue house from the inside, and for those of us who are trying to understand it from the outside.

This is your story and I am honored to tell it.

When I met the one I wanted to marry,
we started building a house.

At first it was small and red,
like passion and roses and warmth
and the little heart we used to write, "I 🤍 you."

We each had our own closet,
added rooms when the children were born,
and a front porch when we retired.

But he moved out the day he died and
left everything he owned behind.

Including me.

He did not own me, but I was still his
and he was still mine. Everything is
different now . . . except for that.

After it happened it felt as if our little red house
had been painted blue by tiny unseen fairies,
beckoned by grief under the cover of night.

Not only that, but it was also moved into a
new neighborhood with unfamiliar streets,
on the corner of Always and Never Again.

The rules inside our house changed too.
Now I have to make the bed and get my own drink of water.
I eat granola bars for dinner, wash my own cup,
and lock the house up at night. *All by myself.*

But the furniture is still the same old furniture,
only a little more tear-stained and one size too big.
Sometimes I sleep better when I lie sideways
on our bed. I don't know why.

I have bought very little since he died.

I guess most things have simply lost their charm.

But I saw a clock I just had to have.
It says, "Now, now, now,"
because later may never come.

It reminds me of the one I love because that's how he lived.

If I could only hear him, I am certain he
would be urging me to live the same way now.

I tell my new neighbors that I miss
my old neighborhood. They encourage me to
remember the good times I had there.

I do not like my new neighbors.

They are just too full of good advice.
I hope I will learn to like them, though, because all
my couple friends seem to have disappeared.

Is it possible they don't know my new address?

I did not realize how many people I was
actually going to lose when my husband died.
I am glad I didn't know.

Some days our house feels too big
and some days it feels like the walls are closing in.

The lights and heater go out without warning.

My favorite electrician says there must be
a loose connection somewhere. He knows,
because his house does the same thing.

I do my best to be "okay"
and even manage to feel good on some days.

But trying to be okay is
like sitting on top of a leaning fence.

It is easier to fall off than stay on.

And just because I have good days does not mean
my little blue house disappeared—

or that I don't cry in the driveway

or have to walk through the front door every night.

Sometimes I send myself flowers
just so there is something nice to come home to.

Even if I move, fall in love again,

or build a new house,

the little blue house is inside of me—*still.*

Even though we had never built a house before,
it is ridiculously indestructible.

Don't ask me how I know. . .

Okay.

The truth is, I have tried to burn it down.

More than once.

I would have done anything to be rid of it.

I want to blame him.

I never would have done anything like that
if he were still alive.

He would have talked me out of it.

I miss my old self—the more beloved, more confident,
    less vulnerable, less afraid, and less crazy me.

When he was here I knew if I got it wrong,
        he would make it right again.

He would catch whatever I missed.

Ughhh. The stakes feel higher than ever.
Now I am like a catcher without a backstop.

The game is tied and the bases are loaded . . .

But unfortunately I am not at a baseball game.
I am in my little blue house
that will not burn and I cannot sell.

Wouldn't you know it? The deed is non-transferable.

Funny thing, though.

There's a cryptic line in small print at the bottom that
says something about redeeming my little house
for a mansion upon my death.

(I really hope so because I am counting on it.)

REDEEMED

Sometimes I think I hate my house now
as much as I loved it before.

But you know something?
I would build it exactly the same if I had
the chance to do it all over again.

Exactly the same.

But I still do not open the door to his closet.

I keep using and washing the same
set of sheets over and over and over because
the other ones are in *there*.

I try to have people over when I can.

Some guests are better than others.

But Mr. Loneliness is the *worst*.

He just lets himself in, sits on the couch, and chain smokes. I can hardly breathe when he comes.

He doesn't seem to care if I am there or not.

So I usually go for a walk.

Sometimes I wonder if he is blind because he simply
does not look at me. He just stares straight ahead.

I prod him with questions but he never speaks.
Or accepts a cup of tea.

He just sits there, looking glum. And smokes.

Sometimes I want to poke him with a sharp stick just
to see what he will do. Thankfully, he doesn't stay forever—

but he *always* stays too long.

Even though Mr. Loneliness is a mystery to me,
I have noticed a pattern. I think he is a sports fan because
he always seems to be around when the Aggies play—
whether I go to the game or watch it on TV.

He follows me into church, lingers on birthdays, holidays,
and the days before the dreaded D-Day.

He pops in after I hear a love song and camps out
in my husband's chair when we should be
toasting ourselves on our anniversary.

But he seems to find particular enjoyment
in coming out of nowhere.

Like when I am surrounded by people,
see an elderly couple holding hands,
or am enjoying a beautiful sunset.

I never like him,

but I like him least of all then.

Before I know it, I have locked all the doors,
shut the lights off, and climbed into bed.

I don't even hear the phone ring.

If it is ringing at all.

But morning comes.

When the sun shines through the window,
I notice that I can smile when I talk to his picture.

You know, the one that hangs at 6'1"—his very height.
So I can kiss him in the hallway before
I go to bed every night

and again the next morning,

before facing the day without him.

No one wants to hear it (well, I certainly didn't),
but a new day and a little time really do
make little-blue-house life a
teensy-weensy bit more bearable.

The morning sun seems to sweeten the
memories that were so bitter the day before
and melts the ice that clung to them in
the cool darkness of fresh grief.

You can still cry at the drop of a hat,
but you can laugh too.

Over time you can add on,
change the curtains,
and spend some time in the garden.

And you can still make beautiful things.

On a good day you can even lose track of time
in your garage, your sewing room, or your art studio.

I am learning that other people have little blue houses too.

Same story with different builders and floor plans.

We recognize each other right away.

And somehow you feel better and
safer just knowing they exist.

But the thing is,
no one can live with someone who
lives in a little blue house.

Except the other person who helped build it—
the one who went away.

So that will always feel a little bit lonely.

My friends say having a dog helps.

Maybe.

But for now I am thinking about
adding on a sunroom and some skylights . . .
for when the power goes out.

Watching the birds at the bird feeder brings me peace.

They remind me that I too am being provided for.

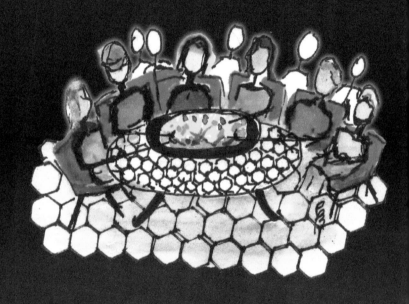

Sometimes I like to have a fire in my fire pit.

Especially at night.

I like to watch the flames dance before they
disappear to nourish the life of the glowing embers.

The warmth pervades my soul and
I am as comforted as I am mesmerized by it.

I like to do this alone as much as with my friends.

The only problem is that they cannot all fit
around the fire pit at the same time.

So they take turns.

Going to the gym and getting together
with my friends helps my grief muscles grow stronger.

And that is good, because grief does not care
how much it weighs.

I am learning that I feel better when I am
serving others and being productive.

I need to be reminded that I am still needed
and valuable and that the world is bigger
than me and my little blue house.

Of course, if I don't feel like staying home
I can always leave.

I can carry out the plans we made together
or go solo with a brand-new map.

I can go on a cruise or volunteer at a food bank,
hospice, or with the scouts.

Find someone else who lives in a little blue house
and make a coffee date or share some chicken noodle soup.

But whether I go or whether I stay,

whether it is rainy, sunny, or gray,

whether I cross the ocean or just the hallway—

the little blue house will be tucked

inside my big red heart,

still.

And really—that is good, because it is mine.

Like a friend who knows the whole story.

After spending so much time together, well . . .

I would feel a little homeless without it.

But I am not homeless.

I live alone in a little blue house.

I did not choose it.

I never, *ever* would have chosen it.

But you have to play the hand you're dealt, they say.

Well, I *am* playing it.

And life in the little blue house will never
be the same as life before it.

It will never be the same,
and it is not something to get *over*.

Getting over the very best and
the very worst
thing that ever happened to you?

(Can you imagine?)

But living with it,
through it,
in it,
and forward
is still possible.

Life . . .

even life in a little blue house . . .

can still be (very) good.

Wanna come over?

ACKNOWLEDGMENTS

Special thanks to Pam for beloved "neverness" and the red door; Mickey for the clock; Jeanette for the drink of water; Cathy for editing and for the cup; Penny for the granola bars; Jeanne for locking up at night; David for the electrician help; Helen for the fence; Carey for the sheets; Jon for sleeping sideways; Judy for Mr. Loneliness and the flowers; Phyllis for the Aggies; Sid for the backstop; Melanie for the picture hung at husband height; Rita for the gym; Karen for the cruises; Totsy, Leonette, Maria, Carol, Rose Marie, Rita, Wayne, and Jon for serving; Earl for chicken noodle soup; everybody for my fire pit and taking turns; and Coleen for every picture from beginning to end.

EPILOGUE

After hearing their story, the members of our group wanted to leave some thoughts for you or messages for their spouses:

No matter how long you are with your spouse,
it is never enough.
—Arline R.

We share what is precious to us and find courage
for the days to come.
—Maria A.

Hug and kiss your spouse, because you never
know when it will be the last time.
—Judy R.

No matter the structure of your house,
whether it's made of solid steel, wood, or brick,
it will always be your home.
—Melissa W.

My house just feels like a house now. Terri made it
our home. She had a heart as big as Texas.
—Carey W.

I'm still trying to be the man Regina knew I was all along.
—Kirk E.

Memories can bring tears—and in time,
laughter. I never wanted to be on this grief journey.
I know he would want me to be happy.
—Sally L.

I was blessed.
—Jan D.

"Once the storm is over, you won't remember how
you made it through, how you managed to survive.
You won't even be sure whether the storm is really over.
But one thing is certain. When you come out of
the storm, you won't be the same person who
walked in." Here's to "all things becoming new."
—Favorite quote of Pam S.

Part of my morning prayers: God, Jesus, help me.
You have always been with me. I have always known
you, talked to you, and depended on you. When I was of
a certain age, I was lonely. You blessed me with the gift
of Sandie. I was no longer lonely. I was complete. I still
loved you. Sandie and I both loved you and worshiped
you together. Life was great. Then you took her away, and
I am lonely again. I am perforated. Of course I still love
you, my creator, but I am lonely again. So now I still have
you, and some new friends like me, but I'm lonely again.
My house echoes with emptiness. Still the same color on
the outside, but very quiet and very dark on the inside.
There are no lights in the windows. I suppose it is like me.

Same color on the outside, although a bit worn, cracked,
and faded. But very quiet and very dark on the inside.
It is so empty, quiet, and dark. So Jesus, I really would
like to hear your voice on the inside. And God, your
light, whatever the color, would be a most welcome sight.
Maybe I am asking too soon. But this wretched earth
creature is anxiously waiting. Not much of a
prayer is it? But it is just another day.
—Jon B.

She was the "Wind Beneath My Wings." Now I feel
grounded, but with God's hand I will rise to her one day.
Yes, when I see her again, I'll say, "I'd Choose You
Again"! These were our two favorite songs for each other.
—Earl M.

Life was special because of his love.
Make today count—tomorrow it will be gone.
—Sharon F.

I thought we had many more tomorrows,
but then I woke up without him at my side.
There is never enough time.
—Cathy A.

Shirley, I love you.
—Wayne P.

Ken, my dreams came true when I married you.
—Rita B.

Rugg, you gave my life the meaning I searched for my whole life. Now I struggle because I miss you even though I know you are in paradise with our Lord and Savior.

—Penny R.

A prayer I say often: Dear Lord, I accept that this grief will always be with me and trust in you that you will help me manage it. Please give me the strength to use the gifts you have given me to honor the memory of my husband and to help others find friendship and support during this time of sorrow and loss. I place my trust in you, Lord. Amen.

—Coleen B.

Heidi Dixon is a wife, mother, hospice chaplain, grief support group facilitator, and graduate student. She will graduate in December 2024 with a master's degree in education in marriage, couples, and family counseling from Lamar University. This is her first book.

Coleen Bradfield is an intuitive color artist who enjoys mixed media painting and sculpting. She was married to Jay Bradfield and is a mother and grandmother. Her work is exhibited in galleries and homes throughout the United States, Germany, and Austria.

Coleen continues being a strong supporter of the arts in her community and is a studio artist at the Brazos Valley Arts Council Gallery of Fine Arts and Visitors Center. This is her first book. You can learn more at www.artbycoleen.com.

Heidi and Coleen met when Coleen was caring for her husband, Jay, on his cancer journey. Heidi was later their hospice chaplain and relished the highest honor of singing an original song co-written by Jay at his celebration of life. Coleen is a faithful member of the "Until We Meet Again" grief support group for spouses, which inspired this book.

Follow us on Facebook and join the conversation at
www.mylittlebluehouse.com.

Printed in the USA
CPSIA information can be obtained
at www.ICGtesting.com
LVHW050054030224
770532LV00001B/1